BLOWJOB

How to become a world-class BLOWJOB QUEEN

by
JACK DICK

This book is for all the ladies out there who should improve their blowjob skills and eventually become a world-class blowjob queen.

The book provides you with a proven and easy to practice guideline to improve your blowjob skills.

PRACTICE EVERY DAY

PRACTICE EVERY DAY

PRACTICE EVERY DAY

PRACTICE EVERY DAY

DID YOU PRACTICE TODAY?

PRACTICE EVERY DAY

PRACTICE EVERY DAY

PRACTICE EVERY DAY

PRACTICE EVERY DAY

PRACTICE EVERY DAY

PRACTICE EVERY DAY

PRACTICE EVERY DAY

PRACTICE EVERY DAY

PRACTICE EVERY DAY

PRACTICE EVERY DAY

PRACTICE EVERY DAY

PRACTICE EVERY DAY

PRACTICE EVERY DAY

PRACTICE EVERY DAY

PRACTICE EVERY DAY

PRACTICE EVERY DAY

PRACTICE EVERY DAY

PRACTICE EVERY DAY

PRACTICE EVERY DAY

›*PRACTICE EVERY DAY*

PRACTICE EVERY DAY

PRACTICE EVERY DAY

PRACTICE EVERY DAY

PRACTICE EVERY DAY

PRACTICE EVERY DAY

PRACTICE EVERY DAY

PRACTICE EVERY DAY

PRACTICE EVERY DAY

PRACTICE EVERY DAY

PRACTICE EVERY DAY

PRACTICE EVERY DAY

PRACTICE EVERY DAY

PRACTICE EVERY DAY

I TOLD YOU TO PRACTICE!

PRACTICE EVERY DAY

PRACTICE EVERY DAY

PRACTICE EVERY DAY

PRACTICE EVERY DAY

PRACTICE EVERY DAY

YES, EVERY DAY!

PRACTICE EVERY DAY

PRACTICE EVERY DAY

PRACTICE EVERY DAY

PRACTICE EVERY DAY

PRACTICE EVERY DAY

PRACTICE EVERY DAY

PRACTICE EVERY DAY

PRACTICE EVERY DAY

PRACTICE EVERY DAY

PRACTICE EVERY DAY

PRACTICE EVERY DAY

PRACTICE EVERY DAY

PRACTICE EVERY DAY

PRACTICE EVERY DAY

PRACTICE EVERY DAY

ESPECIALLY TODAY!

PRACTICE EVERY DAY

PRACTICE EVERY DAY

PRACTICE EVERY DAY

PRACTICE EVERY DAY

PRACTICE EVERY DAY

PRACTICE EVERY DAY

PRACTICE EVERY DAY

PRACTICE EVERY DAY

PRACTICE EVERY DAY

PRACTICE EVERY DAY

PRACTICE EVERY DAY

PRACTICE EVERY DAY

PRACTICE EVERY DAY

PRACTICE EVERY DAY

PRACTICE EVERY DAY

PRACTICE EVERY DAY

PRACTICE EVERY DAY

PRACTICE EVERY DAY

PRACTICE EVERY DAY

PRACTICE EVERY DAY

PRACTICE EVERY DAY

PRACTICE EVERY DAY

PRACTICE EVERY DAY

PRACTICE EVERY DAY

PRACTICE EVERY DAY

PRACTICE EVERY DAY

PRACTICE EVERY DAY

PRACTICE EVERY DAY

PRACTICE EVERY DAY

PRACTICE EVERY DAY

PRACTICE EVERY DAY

PRACTICE EVERY DAY

PRACTICE EVERY DAY

PRACTICE EVERY DAY

PRACTICE EVERY DAY

PRACTICE EVERY DAY

PRACTICE EVERY DAY

PRACTICE EVERY DAY

PRACTICE EVERY DAY

PRACTICE EVERY DAY

PRACTICE EVERY DAY

PRACTICE EVERY DAY

PRACTICE EVERY DAY

PRACTICE EVERY DAY

PRACTICE EVERY DAY

PRACTICE EVERY DAY

PRACTICE EVERY DAY

PRACTICE EVERY DAY

PRACTICE EVERY DAY

PRACTICE EVERY DAY

PRACTICE EVERY DAY

PRACTICE EVERY DAY

PRACTICE EVERY DAY

PRACTICE EVERY DAY

PRACTICE EVERY DAY

PRACTICE EVERY DAY

PRACTICE EVERY DAY

PRACTICE EVERY DAY

PRACTICE EVERY DAY

PRACTICE EVERY DAY

PRACTICE EVERY DAY

PRACTICE EVERY DAY

PRACTICE EVERY DAY

PRACTICE EVERY DAY

PRACTICE EVERY DAY

PRACTICE EVERY DAY

PRACTICE EVERY DAY

PRACTICE EVERY DAY

PRACTICE EVERY DAY

PRACTICE EVERY DAY

PRACTICE EVERY DAY

PRACTICE EVERY DAY

PRACTICE EVERY DAY

PRACTICE EVERY DAY

PRACTICE EVERY DAY

PRACTICE EVERY DAY

PRACTICE EVERY DAY

SOON YOU WILL BE A REAL BLOWJOB QUEEN

PRACTICE EVERY DAY

PRACTICE EVERY DAY

PRACTICE EVERY DAY

PRACTICE EVERY DAY

PRACTICE EVERY DAY

PRACTICE EVERY DAY

PRACTICE EVERY DAY

PRACTICE EVERY DAY

PRACTICE EVERY DAY

PRACTICE EVERY DAY

PRACTICE EVERY DAY

PRACTICE EVERY DAY

PRACTICE EVERY DAY

PRACTICE EVERY DAY

PRACTICE EVERY DAY

PRACTICE EVERY DAY

PRACTICE EVERY DAY

PRACTICE EVERY DAY

PRACTICE EVERY DAY

Made in the USA
Middletown, DE
03 July 2025

10083171R00089